ELEMENTARY LIBRARY
HESPERIA COMMUNITY SCHOOLS
96 S. DIVISION
HESPERIA, MI 49421

Tales of Heaven and Earth

Amina Okada is a specialist
in the art and civilization of India,
and a curator at the Musée National
des Arts Asiatiques-Guimet in Paris.
She is the author of several books about India.

Cover design by Peter Bennett

Published by Creative Education
123 South Broad Street, Mankato, Minnesota 56001
Creative Education is an imprint
of The Creative Company

Copyright © 1993 Editions Gallimard
English text © 1995 Moonlight Publishing Ltd.
International copyrights reserved in all countries.
No part of this book may be reproduced in any form
without written permission from the publisher.
Printed in Italy.

Library of Congress Cataloging-in-Publication Data

Okada, Amina.
[Le prince qui se fit mendiant. English]
The prince who became a beggar / by Amina Okada;
illustrated by Dominique Thibault;
translated by Gwen Marsh.
p. cm. — (Tales of heaven and earth)
Summary: Recounts the story of Prince Siddhartha and how he
became Buddha, the Enlightened One.
ISBN 0-88682-828-7

1. Gautama Buddha—Juvenile literature.
I. Thibault, Dominique, ill. II. Marsh, Gwen. III. Title. IV. Series.
BQ892.033   1997
294.3'63—dc20   96-27643
[B]

6 5 4 3 2 1

The Prince Who Became a Beggar

by Amina Okada
Illustrated by Dominique Thibault
Translated by Gwen Marsh

Creative Education

Two and a half–thousand years ago, in a small Himalayan kingdom . . .

The Buddha was born at Kapilavastu, in what is now Nepal in the foothills of the high Himalayas. This mountain range of some 1,740 miles, stretching from India to China, is the highest in the world. Mount Everest, the topmost peak, is 29,030 feet high.

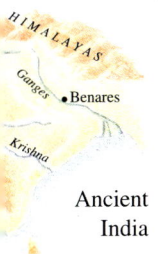

Ancient India

The *apsaras* are divine water nymphs. By their grace and beauty, they trouble and bewitch both men and gods.

This story begins 2,500 years ago in Kapilavastu, in the north of India in the foothills of the Himalayas. Here King Shuddhodana reigned over a small, prosperous kingdom below peaks that are always covered in snow, winter and summer alike. The king was wise, just, and good; and his wife was Queen Maya, whose beauty dazzled like lightning and made the legendary grace of the nymphs, the heavenly *apsaras,* seem dull beside her.

One night, in the season of rains, when the moon was full, Queen Maya saw in a dream a little elephant

5

descend upon her  from the sky and melt into her right side. He was white except for his head, which was as red as cochineal, and he had six tusks. The queen told King Shuddhodana of her strange dream and he consulted the court astrologer as to its meaning.

The astrologer gave it much thought and at last declared that the dream foretold a happy event. "O king, Queen Maya will soon bear a son who will be a lion among men. He will be either a great king whose reign will be known for justice, not war or punishment, or he will be the greatest sage if he renounces the throne and devotes himself to the search for truth."

The king and queen rejoiced, sure that their son would be the most worthy of monarchs. Ten months passed; it

Astrologers and seers were important in the social life of ancient India. Every Indian sovereign kept several astrologers at his court. He would consult with them before any important decision or event to make sure that the stars were favorable.

Cochineal is the name of a variety of insect. The females provide a dye of rich red, or carmine.

The season of the rains is known as the *monsoon* (a word meaning season). The southwest wind, which blows in June in north India, brings rain necessary for the crops. Thousands would die from famine if the rains failed.

. . . the Prince Siddhartha is born.

was the time of the full moon in May. The Lumbini garden was full of birdsong and softly carpeted with flowers, and Queen Maya felt an urge to walk there.

The queen wandered among the trees, admiring the fresh leaves and bursting buds and creepers full of sap. Suddenly her eyes fell on a tree draped with supple climbing plants and young shoots, whose lower branches seemed to be bowing gracefully to her. The queen raised her arm to pluck one of the branches and the child in her belly was born gently from her right side without hurting her. The gods Indra and Brahma received the newborn baby as he came from his mother's side, and wrapped him in a divine cloth. Two flower-scented showers, one cold and one warm, fell from heaven to give him his first bath. Then, freeing himself from the gods who held him, the child took seven steps to the north and turned to look toward the four cardinal points, thus affirming his future sovereignty over the world.

Indra is the god of the sky, of thunder and lightning—the chief god in ancient Hinduism. He rides the elephant Airavata.

Brahma, with Shiva and Vishnu, is one of the three main gods of Hinduism, and the creator of the universe. He is represented with four heads, and rides a wild goose, or *hamsa*.

Seven is a holy number symbolizing perfection. It evokes the union of the earth (represented by the number four) with heaven (represented by the number three).

Brahmins are the men who perform Hindu rituals and pass on knowledge of the sacred texts and rites.

His body bears the signs that mark a person destined for greatness.

The thirty-two distinctive signs of an eminent man (a world famous monarch or Buddha) were proof of the merit acquired during his previous lives.

Chakra is a Sanskrit word (the ancient language of India) meaning wheel. The *chakra* stands for the Wheel of the Law, the symbol of the teaching that the Buddha would bring to people.

Back in the palace the Brahmins and seers examined the baby and confirmed that his body bore the thirty-two signs that single out from the common people one who is destined to be great. The child had a tuft of hair between the eyes and a bump on his head with hair that formed a sort of bun. His fingers were webbed and the palms of his hands and the soles of his feet bore the print of the Wheel of the Law—the Dharma *chakra*. Everyone at the court was sure that the prince Siddhartha—for that was the name he was given—would become a famous king known around the world.

Throughout the realm there was celebration for the birth. But the palace was struck with sadness when, seven days later, Queen Maya died. Siddhartha was brought up by his mother's sister until he was seven years old. Then a master taught him the sixty-four arts taught to princes. He enjoyed study and was equally clever at grammar, music, and math. He excelled at chess, wrestling, and the

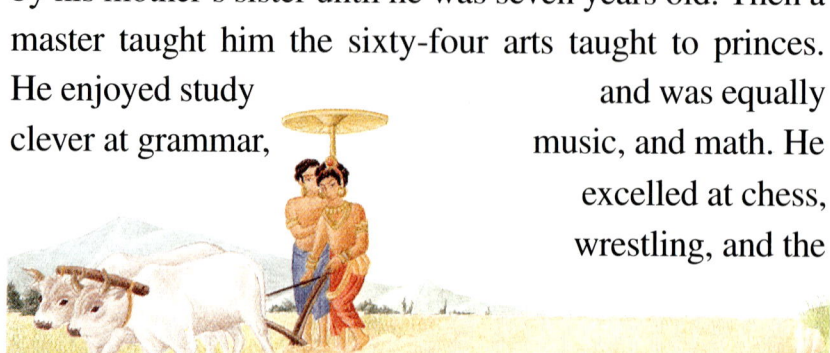

Siddhartha means "He who has reached his goal." He will be called the *Buddha,* the Awakened One, when he attains Enlightenment. He will also be called *Shakyamuni,* the Sage of the Shakya, having been born into the warrior clan of the Shakya.

Will he be a famous king or the greatest of sages?

use of arms. He helped his father to deal out justice, for the young prince was wise beyond his years.

One day, King Shuddhodana took Siddhartha with him to a peasant village at ploughing time—it was the custom for the king to plough the first furrow. The prince sat down under a rose-apple tree to watch the ceremony. He saw the backbreaking toil and sweat of the men in the scorching sun, the oxen straining at the yoke, and the earth splitting as the ploughshare shredded roots, plants, and small creatures. He noticed an ant that a lizard had just caught with a flick of the tongue, and then saw how a snake in its turn ate the lizard and how a vulture swooped down and carried off the snake in its talons. Siddhartha meditated for a long time on the suffering of all living things, and his heart was full of sadness and compassion.

The morning wore on; the sun continued on its course through the sky, but the shade of the rose-apple tree stayed still and went on sheltering the prince.

The rite of the first furrow affirms the king's sovereignty, and symbolizes making the earth fertile. Similarly, Romulus in ancient Rome used a plough to mark the boundaries of the city, and Chinese emperors marked the start of a reign by ploughing a furrow in the earth.

Compassion, inspired by the sufferings of living things, moved the future Buddha to set off on his search. This compassion forms the basis of the Buddhist ideal.

By the king's orders, the prince must know only pleasures and delights.

Shuddhodana had only this one son as his successor to the throne. Besides, to become a great king was finer, in his eyes, than to quest for wisdom.

Siddhartha's sadness had not escaped the king's notice. He feared that the seer's prediction might come to pass and that his son might renounce the throne, preferring the path of wisdom to becoming king. "Love would make the prince forget his sadness, overcome his melancholy," declared the king's councilors. "Isn't he sixteen now? It is time for him to take a wife."

A great feast was held in the palace to which all the most beautiful young girls were invited. Wearing their richest apparel, with jewels and the most delicate flowers,

At sixteen he marries Yasodhara, lovely as a lotus flower.

In India, the lotus flower is admired above all others. A symbol of purity for Buddhists, it is also the attribute of several Hindu gods and goddesses.

they came before the prince, who gave each of them a present. The last to appear before Siddhartha was named Yasodhara; her face was radiant like the full moon in autumn, her eyes were like lotus petals, and her dark hair was as silky and lustrous as a peacock's plumage.

Yasodhara was so beautiful that Siddhartha decided at once to take her as his wife. However, to obtain her hand he had to submit to a series of sporting contests in which 500 young princes competed. Siddhartha showed his strength at drawing the bow and he broke all the bows brought to him, eventually using one that was so heavy that no one else had been able to use it.

Victorious, he married Yasodhara and passed the days happily with his wife in the soft and carefree life of the palace, enjoying the amusements and pleasures that are the privilege of princes. After thirteen years of marriage, when Siddhartha was just twenty-nine, Yasodhara bore a son, Rahula.

The king felt reassured. He believed that his son

Siddhartha managed to draw the bow of his ancestor, which was kept in a temple. It was too heavy for anyone to lift. The arrow that he shot went through several targets, and where it struck the earth a spring gushed forth.

11

His life seems one long enchantment until the day when . . .

would never renounce the throne now. He arranged for the prince's life to be an ocean of delight in which he would be spared any sight of the world's misery or sadness. Then, one day, the prince left the palace with his faithful squire, Chandaka, and rode down to the town. As he rode through the park along paths lined with trees and flowers, Siddhartha noticed an old man with a wrinkled face and a bent back, who walked painfully, leaning on a stick.

"Who is that man?" the prince asked Chandaka. "Why is his body so bent and why does he totter? Why is his hair as white as snow and not as black as ebony?"

"He's an old man, Lord; it is many long years since he was young and strong; he won't live much longer."

"Shall I too be like that old man one day?"

"Yes, Lord," replied Chandaka, lowering his eyes. "Every person in this world has to grow old."

To overcome the suffering bound to the human condition, Prince Siddhartha decided to renounce the world and search for truth. The truth he sought was how to overcome sufferings by understanding their cause and their true nature.

. . . he discovers old age . . .

Hearing these words, the prince's heart was filled with a deep sadness and all the pleasure of the ride vanished.

"That's enough for today. Let's go back to the palace!" he said to Chandaka.

Some time after that, Siddhartha again gave orders to his faithful squire to prepare his little chariot to take him into town. As they turned into the park, the prince noticed a man who was breathing painfully and shivering so much that his frail and wasted body shook violently.

"Who is that man, Chandaka? Why are there tears in his eyes? Why does he look so parched with thirst?"

"He is ill, Lord. That man is not likely to recover."

"Shall I too suffer such a fate?" asked the prince.

"Certainly, Lord. Man can no more escape illness than old age."

The prince looked somber as he turned back to the palace, sad at heart.

Some time after this, Siddhartha again sent for his chariot and went out through the west gate of the town. On the way, he noticed a group of men weeping as they carried a corpse on a bier.

"Who is that person lying so still, Chandaka? His face

13

Indians do not bury their dead; they burn them on funeral pyres. According to tradition, the ashes of the one who died will be taken away after the cremation and scattered on the purifying waters of the Ganges or some other sacred river.

is like wax and his eyes are closed to the world."

"That is a dead man, Lord, being carried to the cremation pyre by his family and friends, for his days are over. Breath and spirit have departed, he is no longer conscious of anything and he is lost forever to those he loved."

"Shall I too come to this terrible end?" asked the prince.

"Certainly, Lord. No one is out of reach of death, for it comes to rich and poor alike, to kings as to peasants."

As they were riding back to the palace, Siddhartha saw a man dressed in a long saffron-colored robe. His head and face were shaven and he carried a begging bowl in his hand. He looked calm, his eyes clear and serene.

"That man is different from others, Chandaka. Who is he?"

"He is a religious man, Lord, and a wanderer. He has tamed his passions and always behaves patiently and compassionately toward all creatures. Whatever the circumstances, his manner is dignified, worthy, and

Monks and certain ascetics shave their hair, beards, and mustaches and wear robes of saffron, a color associated with renunciation and saintliness. They beg for their food: this gives everyone who provides them with a meal the chance to acquire merit for their future life.

. . . then illness and death. His meeting with a monk gives him hope again.

In ancient India, a person's life was ideally divided into four stages. The first was devoted to acquiring knowledge; the second to marriage and family; the third to dwelling in the forest; and the last to the life of a wanderer. In this last stage, a man would try to free himself from all ties that bound him to earthly things.

benevolent. He has left his home so as to dedicate himself solely to a religious life."

Siddhartha listened with the liveliest interest to what Chandaka said. His eyes shone and he felt a weight lifted from his heart.

Back in the palace, Siddhartha was overwhelmed by a deep distaste for all the riches piled up in his coffers and the entertainments offered him. How self-indulgent, pointless, and idle his life was! That night, he went into the women's quarters, sat on his wife's couch, and contemplated the sleeping Yasodhara clasping little Rahula in her arms.

"How shall I ever be able to leave these two precious beings who love me so much and whom I love even more?" thought the prince. But he knew that he had made a decision and his will would hold firm. He turned and saw then the musicians and servants sleeping in the next room. Their instruments lay on the floor in disorder and their clothes were rumpled. They must have dropped exhausted where they stood after a night of feasting and dancing, and they slept with their mouths open, dribbling and snoring.

Queens, princesses, and women of high rank lived in apartments of their own. Men from outside the family were not admitted.

He makes his decision: he too will try to find the cure for suffering.

Music is closely linked to the life of a princely court in India, and is considered to be divine in its nature. Among familiar instruments the *mridanga* (a sort of drum) was often used.

At that moment, Siddhartha felt a wave of revulsion for his luxurious life as a prince and knew that it was time for him to leave the palace. He needed to go in search of truth and to understand at last why death and suffering are always there, lurking behind the outward appearance of things. He had to find the cure for the misery of humanity.

The prince left the women's quarters and called his squire. "Wake up, Chandaka, and harness my horse."

"It's never good to travel at night, Lord," replied his squire. "I don't see any enemies threatening the palace. Why this sudden departure?"

"The enemies, Chandaka, are old age, illness, and death, and I know of no worse enemies to man than

these. So saddle my horse without more delay, for I fear that my people may try to stop us!"

The squire said no more and harnessed the prince's white horse. But just as Siddhartha was about to mount, the animal let out a long, sad neigh—like a sob. Then the gods, who had been watching from the sky and who were protecting the prince's flight, swept away the sound the horse had made so that no one in the sleeping palace would hear it. Quickly, they dispatched to Earth a troop of sprites who held up the animal's legs to silence the sound of thudding hooves as it galloped away.

Silently, Siddhartha rode out of the palace domain, and then through the town, whose heavy gates, as if pushed by the gods themselves, turned miraculously on their hinges to let the prince pass. He rode on all night and in the morning came to a wood. Here he removed his princely clothes, his jewels and earrings, took off his turban and cut off his hair with his sword. The gods

The squire handaka and the horse Kanthaka were both born on the same day as Siddhartha, hence the strong bond between them and their master.

In this picturesque Buddhist legend, the Hindu gods put themselves humbly at the Buddha's service.

17

One night he left the palace to adopt the life of an ascetic.

Homeless wanderers, or *sannyasins,* dress in rags and own nothing but their pilgrim's staff and a begging bowl for their daily food.

gathered this up as a precious relic and carried it away into the sky. Then he turned to the faithful Chandaka, who was sobbing, prostrate at his feet.

"Lead my horse back, take my jewels, and return to the palace. Tell my father, good King Shuddhodana, and my wife, the lovely Yasodhara, that I am leaving them now to follow the path of salvation and I shall not return unless I find the remedy for the sufferings of mankind, even if that means leaving my bones to dry and rot in the desert! Tell them not to be sad but rather to rejoice."

As a prince, Siddhartha wore rich jewels and heavy earrings whose weight stretched the ear lobes. Buddhist art often showed him with long ear lobes as a reminder that he was once a prince.

Enlightenment is the final liberation from the cycle of rebirth.

For five years, Siddhartha . . .

The word *asceticism* means exercise. It refers to strenuous physical or mental exercises which can free the spirit by controlling the body.

Siddhartha followed the teaching of several masters, but none of these wise men could answer his most haunting questions: why is suffering as inescapably attached to us as our own shadow and how can we be free of it?

For some time, he stayed with a sage who taught his disciples, apart from philosophy, severe self-denying practices and mortification of the flesh, so as to subject the body and the senses to the power of the spirit. For five years, Siddhartha gave himself up to these ascetic

The ascetics imposed harsh practices upon themselves to acquire supernatural powers. Such austerity was widely practiced in ancient India. Some ascetics retreated into the forest where they endured hunger and all the hardships of weather; others stayed in unusual postures without moving.

19

. . . subjects himself to the most difficult exercises, especially fasting.

practices nearby the holy place of Gaya, forcing himself to tame his thoughts and control his breathing and gradually give up eating. His food consisted of a few mouthfuls of pea soup or lentils, just a handful of grain or roots. In this way, the young ascetic had grown extremely thin; his arms and legs were like dry reeds, his bones stuck out of his dried-up skin, his face was hollow and fleshless, and the light in his eyes, sunk deep in his skull, was gone, like the reflection of stars in a deep well.

Siddhartha was so weak that one day, when he was going to the river, his legs gave way and he fell on the grass and could not get up. He saw that asceticism was useless if it left the body to waste away and prevented the man from using his ability to learn. He decided to break his fast. He accepted the gift of a dish of rice with milk and honey from a young cowherd's wife, Sujata, and as he ate he felt strength return. Then he bathed in the river, washed his clothes, and went to sit under a pippal tree. A Brahmin cutting grass nearby gave him an armful on which to sit under the tree. Seated under the pippal, his back straight, his

These physical and spiritual exercises—enabling a person to achieve full control of body and thought—are known as *yoga*. Someone who has mastered this discipline is called a *yogi*.

Understanding the futility of excess, he eats and sits down to meditate.

face turned toward the east, his spirit concentrated and clear, he began to meditate, determined to solve the mystery of the human condition.

It was during that night of the full moon in spring that Siddhartha, after meditating at length four times, was to achieve supreme knowledge.

But during that same night—while the gods in heaven were protecting the prince in his quest—Mara, the master of the Shades and Death, decided to fight him without mercy, for he could see that Siddhartha's determination threatened his own power over the world. To disturb the poor sage's meditations, and to prevent him from gaining Enlightenment, Mara dispatched against him armies of monsters, hideous and terrifying. Some were deformed, and their red eyes sparked like the eyes of serpents. Others had goats' ears and repulsive, cruel faces like elephants or wild boars. Others had mountainous bellies, great mouths

According to both Buddhism and Hinduism, human existence is a constant cycle of rebirth. After death, people are born again. The quality of their life depends on their deeds, good or bad, in previous lives. That is karma. Most Indian religious movements try to liberate people from the cycle of death and rebirth and help them enter nirvana.

It was under the pippal tree, or sacred fig tree *(Ficus religiosa)*, that the Buddha himself attained Enlightenment, also called Awakening or Liberation. That means he had reached supreme knowledge beyond all suffering, and was free from the cycle of death and rebirth.

Now he faced the attacks of Mara, master of the Shades...

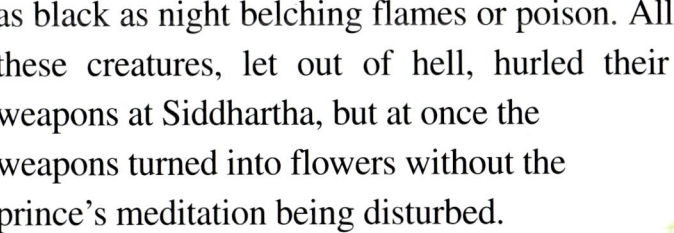

Buddhist art often represents the Buddha sitting under the pippal tree touching the earth with his right hand.

as black as night belching flames or poison. All these creatures, let out of hell, hurled their weapons at Siddhartha, but at once the weapons turned into flowers without the prince's meditation being disturbed.

Seeing this shower of flowers, Mara's fury redoubled. He sent his three daughters—Desire, Pleasure, and Passion—to trouble the sage with their charm and their lascivious dances. But Siddhartha gazed at the three beauties with a look as pure as a diamond and the daughters of Mara changed into decrepit and ugly old women. As a final challenge, Mara tried to break Siddhartha's confidence, suggesting he was not worthy of attaining Enlightenment. As he was alone, with no one to testify to the defeat of Mara, Siddhartha now touched the soil lightly with his fingertips, and the Earth Goddess sprang up as witness to the victory he had just won over the master of Shades and Death.

Thus did Siddhartha meditate all night, and when dawn appeared, touching the sleeping world with fingers of gold, he had achieved supreme knowledge and knew Enlightenment. He had understood that desire is at the source of all pain and that its conquest opens the path to

A symbolic gesture with the hands as performed by Buddhist and Hindu divinities called a *mudra,* a Sanskrit term meaning seal. Gestures are also used by practicing Buddhists and by officiants at rituals. Above is the meditation *mudra.*

When Indian artists represent the Buddha in meditation, they show him seated with his legs crossed, his hands resting on each other palms upward in his lap.

Nirvana or Extinction, denotes the end of rebirths, when all mundane thought, sensation, and passion are extinguished.

23

. . . and at daybreak he has attained the supreme knowledge.

freedom; that the man who has learned to control desire, hatred, and ignorance suffers no more and escapes from the endless chain of rebirth to melt into Nirvana.

He who was no longer the prince Siddhartha but the Buddha—The Enlightened One—remained in meditation for another seven days at the foot of the holy pippal.

One day, when torrential rains struck the region, drowning earth and sky under floods of water, a naga named Mucilinda appeared before the Buddha, gently wrapped its coils around him to keep out the chill and protect him from the rain, and spread its seven heads over him to form a hood. Thus was the Buddha able to continue his meditations in peace, completely indifferent to the flood.

In Indian mythology, *nagas* are snakes (cobras) that guard treasures. Today they are the objects of a popular cult, often linked with trees.

Buddhist wanderers, travelling from place to place preaching, postponed their travel for the monsoon rains from June to September. They stayed in huts built in parks. Many of these places later became Buddhist monasteries.

Having become the Buddha, he began to teach his companions . . .

Having attained Enlightenment, the Buddha decided to teach others the way to free themselves from pain and the cycle of rebirth. He stayed seven weeks in Gaya, then went to Sarnath near the holy city of Benares, where many ascetics and yogis lived. There, in a park where a herd of gazelles lived, the Buddha was reunited with five of his former companions who had followed him when he had adopted the ascetic way of life. In a famous sermon, he shared with them the fruits of his discoveries. These five religious mendicants became his first disciples.

Benares, or Varanasi, built on the banks of the Ganges, is one of the holy cities of India and one of the religious and spiritual centers of Hinduism.

. . . the way to achieve, as he had, absolute transcendence.

The Buddha stayed some time with them. Then, judging that they were competent to teach on their own, he set off on his travels again to bring the Way to Enlightenment to all. He debated with people, explaining and preaching, and resorting to philosophical arguments when he was speaking to educated or religious people. Wherever he passed, there were hosts of converts and many of them shaved their hair and beards, dressed in saffron-colored mendicant robes, and left their homes with nothing but a begging bowl.

The Buddha's prestige was considerable in the middle area of the Ganges valley. It happened sometimes that he performed miracles to prove his superiority over other teachers. This was how he converted to the Buddhist Path three Brahmins who were devotees of a fire cult. These people were called *jatila,* for they wore their hair piled up in a huge bun. In the hut containing the sacrificial fire, a terrible fire-spitting snake had taken refuge.

Agni, the god of fire, is the intermediary between gods and humans when sacrifices are made.

The Buddha began to teach the Buddhist doctrine. It is said that he set the Wheel of the Law rolling. Above is the *mudra* of instruction.

To Hindus, the Ganges is the most sacred river. It flows down from high in the Himalayas for some 1,865 miles before pouring into the Gulf of Bengal, where it forms a vast delta. It flows through the towns of Allahabad, Benares, and Patna.

26

Then, as promised, he returns to his father's palace.

The ascetic subjects himself to hardships and disciplines to gain complete self-control and, in the end, supernatural powers.

The Buddha used his supernatural powers: He tamed the cobra to be like the most inoffensive of grass snakes, and he gave it back to the jatila, curled up in his begging bowl. Then, to impress the Brahmins—who loved such extraordinary feats—he walked dryshod on the swift-flowing river, indifferent to the stormy weather.

But the Buddha had not forgotten his promise to his father and his wife. Six years had passed since he had left the palace by night, and the time had come to preach the doctrine to his own family. The townspeople took a holiday when they heard that the Buddha was coming. And when King Shuddhodana saw his son draped in his saffron robe, his clear eyes pure as a diamond, he understood that the astrologer's prophecy had truly come to pass and that Siddhartha had become the greatest of sages.

After he had preached the Law to his father, the Buddha went into Yasodhara's apartments. At first, she turned

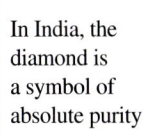

In India, the diamond is a symbol of absolute purity.

away at the sight of the man who had abandoned her and their son Rahula for the path of wisdom. Then, forgetting her bitterness, she prostrated herself at the Buddha's feet; in the end she was content that Rahula should follow his father and become a disciple.

There remained one task that the Buddha was determined to accomplish: to teach the Dharma to his mother, Queen Maya, who had died seven days after his birth. He went up to the heaven of Indra where she had been reborn, and he set out the Dharma to free her from the cycle of rebirth. Then he came back to Earth in India by a triple staircase, escorted by the gods Indra and Brahma.

The Dharma, or Buddhist Teaching and Path, tells what one must do to achieve Enlightenment as the Buddha had done.

The Buddha travels throughout the Ganges valley teaching the Dharma.

The Buddha, the Teaching (Dharma), and the Community of Buddhists (Sangha) form what Buddhists call *The Three Jewels*. On the right, Tibetan painting from the 19th century represents the Buddha with a lotus (the Law) on which a monk is sitting.

For many long years, the Buddha continued his wanderings through the Ganges valley. He used his great abilities, and sometimes his supernatural powers, to convince people of his spiritual supremacy, reminding his faithful followers that good always brings good in its train and that evil can only be followed by evil. Great was his prestige; he had many disciples and the community of his followers was flourishing. However, certain among them, jealous of the Buddha's fame—and such was his cousin Devadatta—cherished a secret desire

29

Then, like all people, he grew old. At 80 he died, liberated . . .

to replace him as head of the community and, to this end, made several attempts on the Master's life. One day, when the Buddha was in the town of Rajagriha, Devadatta—in league with a *cornac*—goaded a furious elephant to rush at him. The beast had caused havoc in the city, uprooting shrubs and shattering everything that came in its way. It was just about to attack the Buddha, who was calmly coming to meet it, when suddenly it stopped, pacified by the serene goodness emanating from the man. With a simple gesture of reassurance, the Master turned aside the elephant's rage and it fell down humbly at his feet.

Forty-five years had gone by since the Enlightenment and the Buddha was now an old man. He was eighty years old and, like other men, he had not escaped old age and illness. He knew that his hour had come, and that death was near with its final deliverance from the chain of rebirths.

He set off on his last journey, to Kushinagara. There, in the heart of a dense

Even when depicting the Buddha at the end of his life, Indian artists traditionally show him with idealized features not marked by age.

The *cornac* is the man charged with caring for and riding an elephant. He has a special crook with which to guide the animal.

This gesture symbolizes protection, the absence of fear. It is made with the right hand raised and open, palm forward.

. . . from rebirth, and enters the peace of nirvana.

teak forest, he gathered all his remaining strength, and spoke to his closest disciple, Ananda, "Prepare a couch for me between those two trees, O Ananda, for I am worn out and I would like to rest."

Ananda spread on the ground a monk's robe folded in two, and the Buddha lay down on his right side with his head to the north and his face to the west. He saw that his companion could hardly hold back his sobs, and the other disciples gathered around him were all in tears. Then he spoke for one last time, "O Ananda, O monks, not one of the countless things that exist in this world can last for ever. Young and old, fools and sages, rich and poor, all are doomed to die. As an earthenware pot is fragile and will break, so is the life of mortals."

Then the Buddha was silent and closed his eyes. He fell into deep meditation and—entering nirvana—breathed his last. His body radiated an extraordinary light and the gods, watching the scene from heaven, cast over him and his community great gilded purple flowers as large as wheels.

The name *Ananda* means beatitude, or happiness.

The death of the Buddha was called *Parinirvana* (or Extinction) because the Buddha, free from the cycle of rebirth, was sure never to be reborn.

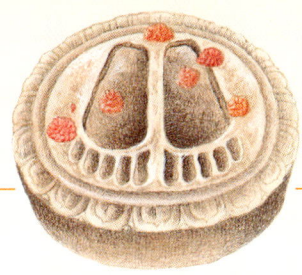

THE LIFE OF BUDDHA

e *kshatriya*—princes and warriors—are embers of the nd of the four reat castes of Hindu society.

These three nimals—pig, cock, and snake—are symbols respectively of ignorance, craving, and ression, three ates that keep ple bound to the cycle of irth. (From a etan painting representing the Wheel of Life.)

The historical person
Born about 560 B.C. at Kapilavastu, Prince Siddhartha was a member of the *kshatriya* caste of the Shakyas and of the Gautama line (hence his name of Gautama Buddha). As a young man, he left his family to be a wandering monk, begging for food and shelter and meditating on suffering, its cause, and how to be free of it.

In meditation, he glimpsed his many previous existences. This confirmed his belief in transmigration, the rebirths of beings after their death. He saw that each life, with its own pleasures and pains, is determined by the moral value of deeds done in past lives (the karma). Having understood the nature and origin of suffering and how to bring it to an end, Siddhartha attained Enlightenment *(Bodhi)* and became the Buddha—the Enlightened One.

For the rest of his life he preached the Buddhist doctrine, travelling through the Ganges valley and gaining many disciples.

He died at Kushinagara in about 480 B.C. after a short illness, and was then said to have entered *Parinirvana,* or Extinction, never to be reborn again. He was finally free forever from the cycle of reincarnation.

How was the legend born?
After his death, many stories were told about the Buddha, based both on historical facts and on imagination. A legend was born, an imaginative and symbolic way of telling the Buddha's story and teachings.

The Buddhist legend grew over time, passed on by the Buddha's disciples and embroidered with moral fables. The story handed down by tradition bears witness to the faith of those who passed it on. It also shows the human tendency to magnify the life and character of important figures.

In a former life, when he was a monkey, the Buddha saved a man's life. Then, when the man attacked him, he converted him.

The earliest representations of the Buddha simply suggest his presence, with an empty throne or his footprints. Those shown above at center are venerated—and decked with flowers from pilgrims—at Bodhgaya, the place of the Enlightenment.

The *Jataka,* or Births, recount the numberless former lives of the Buddha in more than 500 tales. The date of this collection of moral tales is not known. The future Buddha appears here in many forms, animal and human, as a noble creature, kind and always ready to give his life to save others.

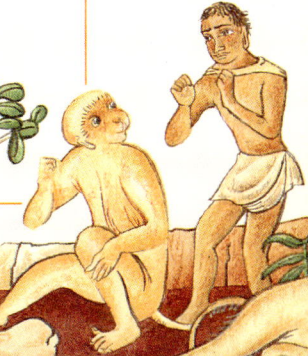

INDIA IN THE 6TH CENTURY B.C.

The ancient civilizations of India first appeared and flourished thousands of years ago, near the Ganges River and its tributary the Yamuna.

The oldest religion
The oldest religion in India is Brahminism, also known as Vedism, the early form of Hinduism based on the holy texts of the *Veda*. These are the world's oldest religious writings. They lay the foundation of Hinduism and give specific instructions for conducting rituals. The *Vedas* gave rise to a religion that emphasized rites and sacrifices to gods who controlled the natural forces of the world.

The caste system
The society founded by the Aryans was strongly hierarchic: it was divided into four great castes, or classes. The highest was the priestly caste, the Brahmins; matters of religion and the performing of rites fell to them. Then came the *kshatriya* caste, made up of kings, nobles, and warriors. Common folk, farmers,

The *Vedas* (sanskrit term that means Knowledge) are looked upon as the wisdom of Brahma (God), as revealed to the sages.

The Yamuna a tributary of Ganges and o of the sacred rivers of India The land that lies between the Ganges an the Yamuna (a region calle Doab, the Tw Rivers) was the cradle of ancient Indian civilization.

The Aryans a pastoral trib from Central Asia. They ca to India abou 1500 B.C. through the northwestern passes, the w that all invade of the subcontinent came in early times. They brought with them their religion, Brahminism, their languag sanskrit, whi remained the language of learning and literature for north of India

and merchants belonged to the *vaicya* caste; servants fell in the lowest caste, the *shudra*. But even the last of these castes had privileges, unlike the outcastes, or Untouchables, whom Gandhi called *harijan*.

Yoga: mastery over the spirit

Brahminism developed toward meditation. The *Upanishads*, written between the 6th and the 3rd centuries B.C., showed new beliefs in the cycles of rebirth and mastery of the spirit through yoga.

Wandering spiritual seekers who renounced all earthly ties chose to leave their place in society in order to attain salvation. Some practiced asceticism as a way to control the vital force of life and acquire supernatural powers.

Two new religions

The 6th century B.C. was, in India, a period of intense spiritual and religious ferment, and two new religions, Buddhism and Jainism, were becoming popular.

Like the Buddha, *Mahavira*—the Great Hero—also called *Jina*, was born into a princely family and led the life of a wandering monk. (The name *Jain* means a disciple of Jina.) But whereas the Buddha recommended a moderate path to finding salvation, Mahavira recommended harsh practices and a severe religious discipline to lead the soul to its liberation.

Jainism

The Jain community is divided into two sects: the *Digambaras*, dressed in space—that is to say, naked—and the *Shvetambaras*, dressed in white. Religious Jains wear a piece of muslin over their mouths to avoid swallowing, and thus killing, insects as they breathe, and they use a brush made of feathers or wool to sweep the ground before them of living things as they walk. This *ahimsa*, or nonviolence, is a core idea of Jainism.

As with Buddhism, this religion was highly critical of Brahmins, who dominated Indian religion, but it also adopted some of their beliefs, such as ideas of karma and rebirth.

Ahimsa, both a Buddhist and Jainist ideal, is nonviolence to humans and animals. At the time of Indian independence, Gandhi championed nonviolence.

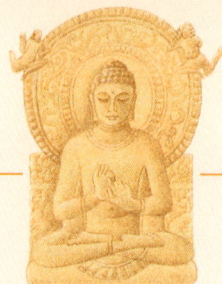

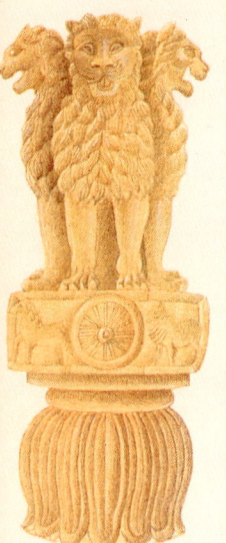

Below: capital of lions at Sarnath. It crowned the 33 foot column built by Asoka in the 3rd century B.C. Above it was the Wheel of the Buddhist Law. It is the symbol of the Indian Union.

Left: the Bud… giving his firs… sermon (sculp… of the 6th cen…

THE TEACHING OF THE BUDDHA

Buddhism began as an ethic, a morality without a god. It gradually changed to become a religion. The Buddha offered a compromise between ascetic self-punishment and the unrestrained pursuit of pleasure. Believing that people's worth depends on their actions, not their birth, Buddhism in India was opposed to the caste system of Brahminism.

Dharma—the Buddhist doctrine

Buddhist doctrine, called Dharma, consists of the Eightfold Path and the Four Noble Truths that the Buddha set out: the reality of suffering, the origin of suffering, the ending of suffering, and the way leading to the ending of suffering.

A basic tenet of Buddhist law is that human desire is the cause of suffering, and all worldly things involve suffering—birth, old age, death, having to live with what you hate, separation from what you love, and not obtaining what you desire. So, if people eliminate desire they can end suffering.

People can train their minds and bodies to abandon the pursuit of pleasure. This can be accomplished by following the Eightfold Path, a moral discipline that helps a person acquire wisdom and progress toward Enlightenment, thus becoming free from the cycle of rebirth.

A moral discipline

In traditionally Buddhist countries, Dharma offers a simple morality for ordinary people living in families and society. The lay Buddhist confirms, in the presence of monks or nuns, acceptance of the doctrine by taking refuge in the Triple Jewel: the Buddha, the Teaching, and the Spiritual Community. Followers are asked to observe the Five Precepts: not to destroy life, not to rob, not to commit adultery, not to lie, not to take any intoxicating drinks.

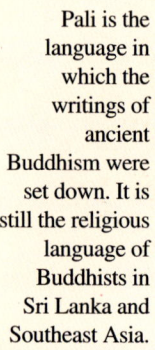

Pali is the language in which the writings of ancient Buddhism were set down. It is still the religious language of Buddhists in Sri Lanka and Southeast Asia.

The life of a Buddhist sho… be ruled by kindness to a… beings, with a… attempt at detachment a… This is necess… if one is to re… the state of Buddha, a sta… of perfect blis…

Monks devot… their lives to spiritual prog… and the teachi… of Buddhism. They observe nonviolence … celibacy.

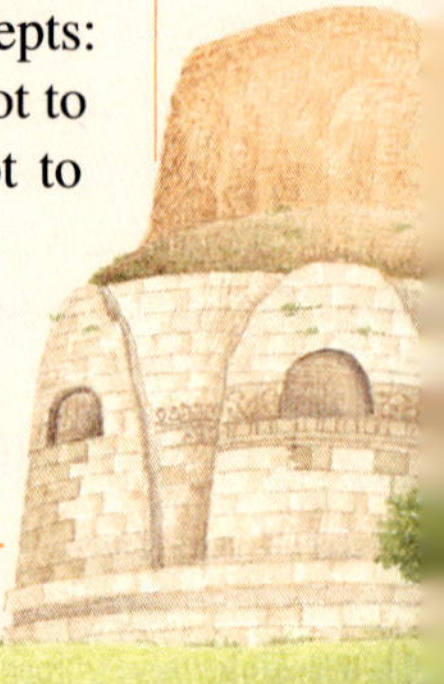

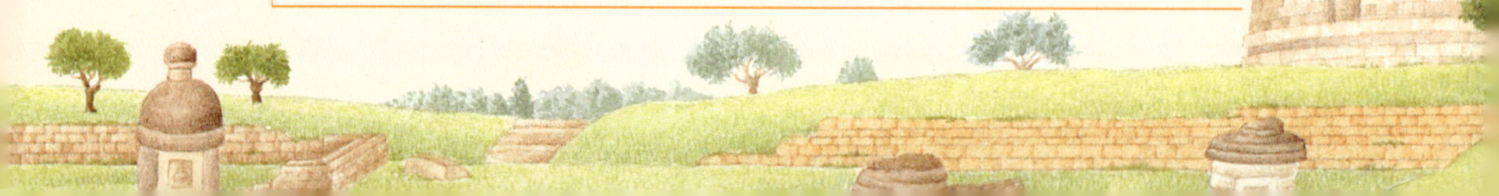

BUDDHIST LITERATURE

Left: the *Parinirvana* (Extinction) of the Buddha, after a bas-relief of the 10th century.

The Buddha died without writing down his teaching. The year after his death there was a council at which all known teachings of the Blessed One were recited and memorized. The teachings were passed on orally for several generations before they began to be written down. These early teachings became the heart of Buddhist Scriptures. Doctrines based on the Buddha's teaching continued to evolve over the centuries.

The Hinayana

The earliest school of Buddhism still surviving is called *Theravada* (way of the Ancients), or *Hinayana*. It is based on the first written Buddhist Scriptures. Among many of the laity, a proper understanding of the Buddha's teaching was gradually replaced by the cult of the Buddha himself, then of relics, and finally the worship of his image, painted or sculpted. In this way Buddhism opened up to popular devotion. Theravada Buddhism attaches great importance to monastic discipline. Its ideal is to attain the state of an *arhat*, a monk who has achieved complete detachment from his passions.

The Mahayana

The more elaborate *Mahayana*, or "Great Vehicle," gradually overtook the Hinayana in India. A cult of the bodhisattas, those destined for Enlightenment, arose. Compassionate beings, they put off the time of their entry into nirvana to help others to salvation. Among popular bodhisattas, Avalokiteshvara protected people, and Maitreya was regarded as the future Buddha.

Below, Mahakala, guardian of the Law, revered by Tibetan Buddhists. His fierce aspect will ensure that the enemies of the Dharma will flee in fright.

White Tara, with seven eyes (on her brow, the palms of her hands, and her feet), is the incarnation of compassion in Tibetan Buddhism.

Center: the bodhisatta Maitreya, a future Buddha, from an 8th century sculpture in bronze.

Gilded *stupas* in Thailand.

The spread of Buddhism

Buddhism was born in India and flourished there from the 3rd century B.C. until the 7th century A.D. Under the Emperor Asoka (3rd century B.C.), who converted to the new doctrine, it began to spread beyond India. He sent out missionaries in all directions. His son, Mahinda, preached in Ceylon, today called Sri Lanka. After that Buddhism became the main religion on that island.

In time, Buddhism reached Southeast Asia (Burma, Laos, Cambodia, Thailand, Vietnam) in the wake of sailors, merchants, and especially, missionaries. It was the *Hinayana* that took hold in these countries. But Buddhism was also gaining along the Silk Road—Central Asia and China, Korea and Japan—where the *Mahayana* dominated. A new variety of Buddhism, known as Tantric, was adopted in Nepal and Tibet, where it has endured.

From the 8th century to the 12th, Buddhism declined in India, then disappeared under the combined assault of the dominant Hinduism and the first waves of Muslim invasion.

However, it is still, today, the second religion of the world (after Christianity) by the number of its followers: more than 600 million in Asia. There are also nearly a million Buddhists spread throughout Europe, North America, and South America.

The spread of Buddhism in the Far East

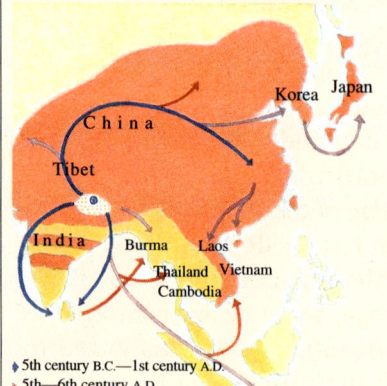

♦ 5th century B.C.—1st century A.D.
▶ 5th—6th century A.D.
● 11th—15th century A.D.
  Hinayana Buddhism
  Mahayana Buddhism

From the 3rd century onwa[rd] travellers wer[e to] India to look [for] manuscripts a[nd] translate them. Above left: th[e] Chinese pilgri[m] Siuan-tsang bringing back many Buddhi[st] texts in the 7th century.

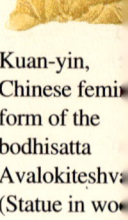

Kuan-yin, Chinese femi[nine] form of the bodhisatta Avalokiteshva[ra.] (Statue in wo[od] from the 13th century.)

The Silk Rou[te] by land and s[ea] in the ancien[t] world connec[ted] the great trad[e,] religious, an[d] cultural cente[rs] of East and West.

BUDDHIST FESTIVALS AND RITES

In Buddhism, rites and ceremonies are thought of as helpful ways of encouraging devotion, not as actual acts of devotion in themselves. Vesak, a festival that goes by many different names, remembers the birth, Enlightenment, and *Parinirvana* of the Buddha. This triple celebration takes place at the full moon in May. Houses and temples are decorated with flowers and lamps and with flags in the six colors of Buddhism.

A tradition of great importance in the lives of Buddhist communities is the *uposatha* which, at the full moon and the new moon, is observed with fasting and strict respect of all religious practices. Devout laypeople pass day and night in the temple, meditating and listening to the teaching of the Dharma.

Baptism doesn't exist in Buddhism, nor does religious marriage, but at births, marriages, or deaths, monks are often asked to participate in symbolic ceremonies. When a person is ill, there may be ceremonies for several days.

The principal holy places
The main events of the Buddha's life took place in Bodhgaya, where he attained Enlightenment, Sarnath, where he gave his first sermon, and Kushinagara, where he entered Nirvana. Today these places are often visited by faithful followers from all over Asia.

The veneration of relics
Relics were parts of the Buddha's body or parts of the body of an important religious person. They were gathered at the place of cremation so that the faithful could worship them, and they were thought to have miraculous powers. They are preserved in urns which are kept in *stupas*.

Left: objects used in rituals— bell, prayer mill (containing holy runes), *vajra*, lamp, and offerings.

In Tibetan Buddhism, certain festivals are celebrated with masked dances performed by the lamas (religious masters).

ayer banners, led *horses of the wind,* are covered with texts whose eficent power arried by the wind to all uarters of the universe.

ditation plays an important part in Zen uddhism, the form that has developed in Japan from Chinese Buddhism.

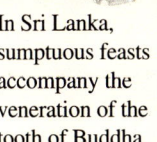

In Sri Lanka, sumptuous feasts accompany the veneration of the tooth of Buddha.

Look for other titles in this series:

THE SECRETS OF KAIDARA
An Animist Tale from Africa

I WANT TO TALK TO GOD
A Tale from Islam

THE RIVER GODDESS
A Tale from Hinduism

CHILDREN OF THE MOON
Yanomami Legends

I'LL TELL YOU A STORY
Tales from Judaism

SARAH, WHO LOVED LAUGHTER
A Tale from the Bible

JESUS SAT DOWN AND SAID . . .
The Parables of Jesus